Good News of Great Joy

Daily Readings for Advent

John Piper

TABLE OF CONTENTS

PREFACE

Advent is for adoring Jesus. At least that's our angle on it at Desiring God.

Advent is an annual season of patient waiting, hopeful expectation, soul-searching, and calendar-watching marked by many churches, Christian families, and individual followers of Jesus. There's no biblical mandate to observe Advent. It's an optional thing—a tradition that developed over the course of the church's history as a time of preparation for Christmas Day. Many of us find observing Advent to be personally enjoyable and spiritually profitable.

The English word "Advent" is from the Latin *adventus*, which means "coming." The advent primarily in view each December is the first coming of Jesus two millennia ago. But Jesus's second coming gets drawn in as well, as the popular Christmas carol "Joy to the World" makes plain:

No more let sins and sorrows grow,
Nor thorns infest the ground;
He comes to make His blessings flow
Far as the curse is found.

Advent begins the fourth Sunday before Christmas and ends Christmas Eve. This means the earliest it begins, depending on where that Sunday falls, is November 27, and the latest it starts is December 3. Whereas Lent (the season of preparation for Easter) is 40 days, Advent ranges in length from 22 to 29 days.

Christians throughout the world have their different ways of celebrating Advent. Some light candles. Some sing songs. Some eat candies. Some give gifts. Some hang wreaths. Many of us do all of the above. Christians have developed many good ways of extending the celebration of Jesus's coming beyond merely the short 24 hours of December 25. The incarnation of the Son of God, "for us and for our salvation," as the old creed says it, is too big a thing to appreciate in just one day. Indeed, it's something the Christian will celebrate for all eternity.

Our prayer is that this little devotional might help you keep Jesus as the center and greatest treasure of your Advent season. The candles and candies have their place, but we want to make sure that in all the December rush and hubbub we adore Jesus above all.

So, "O Come, Let Us Adore Him" is perhaps the theme song of these Advent readings. These meditations are all about adoring Christ, the Lord. In spots, you'll hear strands of "O Come, O Come, Immanuel," and in others, "Hark! The Heralds Angels Sing." And, of course, we'll have a cameo from the magi. But the figure at the center is Jesus—the baby born in Bethlehem, the God-man in swaddling clothes, laid in a manger, destined for Calvary, sent by his Father to die and rise again for his people.

The readings are drawn from the ministry of John Piper, and as always, we encourage you to access more than 30 years of Pastor John's writing and preaching at desiringGod.org. Thanks to Tony Reinke and Jonathan Parnell who helped pull the excerpts.

Also worth noting is that these devotionals correspond with the daily readings from Pastor John in the application called "Solid Joys," which is available for free download in the iTunes store. If you find short daily reflections like these to be helpful, we'd send you to Solid Joys once Advent is done.

The Introduction is designed to be read before the readings begin on December 1. The Conclusion can be read as an additional selection on Christmas Day (or any time before, especially if you're curious about Pastor John's favorite Christmas text). The Appendix on Old Testament shadows and the coming of Christ coordinates with the meditation for December 12 (and you'll find a note in italics there).

May God be pleased to deepen and sweeten your adoring of Jesus this Advent.

David Mathis
Executive Editor
Desiring God

WHAT DOES JESUS WANT THIS CHRISTMAS?

> *"Father, I desire that they also, whom you have given me, may be with me where I am, to see my glory that you have given me because you loved me before the foundation of the world."* —John 17:24

What does Jesus want this Christmas?

We can see the answer in his prayers. What does he ask God for? His longest prayer is John 17. The climax of his desire is in verse 24.

Among all the undeserving sinners in the world, there are those whom God has "given to Jesus." These are those whom God has drawn to the Son (John 6:44, 65). These are *Christians*—people who have "received" Jesus as the crucified and risen Savior and Lord and Treasure of their lives (John 1:12; 3:17; 6:35; 10:11, 17–18; 20:28). Jesus says he wants them to be with him.

Sometimes we hear people say that God created man because he was lonely. So they say, "God created us so that we would be *with him.*" Does Jesus agree with this? Well, he *does* say that he really wants us to be with him! Yes, but why? Consider the rest of the verse. Why does Jesus want us to be with him?

> ... to see my glory that you [Father] have given
> me because you loved me before the foundation of
> the world.

That would be a strange way of expressing his loneliness. "I want them with me so they can see my glory." In fact, it doesn't express his loneliness. It expresses his concern for the satisfaction of *our* longing, not *his* loneliness.

Jesus is not lonely. He and the Father and the Spirit are profoundly satisfied in the fellowship of the Trinity. We, not he, are starving for something. And what Jesus wants for Christmas is for us to experience what we were really made for—seeing and savoring his glory.

Oh, that God would make this sink in to our souls! Jesus made us (John 1:3) to see his glory.

Just before he goes to the cross he pleads his deepest desires with the Father: "Father, I *desire* [I desire!] that they ... may be with me where I am, *to see my glory.*"

But that is only half of what Jesus wants in these final, climactic verses of his prayer. I just said we were really made for seeing *and savoring* his glory. Is that what he wants—that we not only see his glory but savor it, relish it, delight in it, treasure it, love it? Consider verse 26, the very last verse:

I made known to them your name, and I will
continue to make it known, that the love with which
you have loved me may be in them, *and I in them.*

That is the end of the prayer. What is Jesus's *final* goal for us? Not that we simply see his glory, but that we love him with the same love that the Father has for him: "that the love with which you [Father] have loved me may be in them."

Jesus's longing and goal is that we see his glory and then that we be able to love what we see with the same love that the Father has for the Son. And he doesn't mean that we merely *imitate* the love of the Father for the Son. He means the Father's very love becomes our love for the Son—that we love the Son with the love of the Father for the Son. This is what the Spirit becomes and bestows in our lives: Love for the Son by the Father through the Spirit.

What Jesus wants most for Christmas is that his elect be gathered in and then get what *they* want most—to *see* his glory and then *savor* it with the very savoring of the Father for the Son.

What I want most for Christmas this year is to join you (and many others) in seeing Christ in all his fullness and that we together be able to love what we see with a love far beyond our own half-hearted human capacities. This is our goal in these Advent devotionals. We want together to see and savor this Jesus whose first "advent" (coming) we celebrate, and whose second advent we anticipate.

This is what Jesus prays for us this Christmas: "Father, show them my glory and give them the very delight in me that you have in me." Oh, may we *see* Christ with the eyes of God and *savor* Christ with the heart of God. That is the essence of heaven. That is the gift Christ came to purchase for sinners at the cost of his death in our place.

December 1

PREPARE THE WAY

"He will turn many of the children of Israel to the Lord their God, and he will go before him in the spirit and power of Elijah, to turn the hearts of the fathers to the children, and the disobedient to the wisdom of the just, to make ready for the Lord a people prepared." —Luke 1:16–17

What John the Baptist did for Israel, Advent can do for us. Don't let Christmas find you unprepared. I mean *spiritually* unprepared. Its joy and impact will be so much greater if you are ready!

That you might be prepared...

First, meditate on the fact that we need a *Savior*. Christmas is an indictment before it becomes a delight. It will not have its intended effect until we feel desperately the need for a Savior. Let these short Advent meditations help awaken in you a bittersweet sense of need for the Savior.

Second, engage in sober self-examination. Advent is to Christmas what Lent is to Easter. "Search me, O God, and know my heart! Try me and know my thoughts! And see if there be any wicked way in me, and lead me in the way everlasting!" (Psalm 139:23–24) Let every heart *prepare him room*... by cleaning house.

Third, build God-centered anticipation and expectancy and excitement into your home—especially for the children. If you are excited about Christ, they will be too. If you can only make Christmas exciting with material things, how will the children get a thirst for God? Bend the efforts of your imagination to make the wonder of the King's arrival visible for the children.

Fourth, be much in the Scriptures, and memorize the great passages! "Is not my word like fire, says the Lord!" (Jeremiah 23:29) Gather 'round that fire this Advent season. It is warm. It is sparkling with colors of grace. It is healing for a thousand hurts. It is light for dark nights.

December 2

MARY'S MAGNIFICENT GOD

"My soul magnifies the Lord,
and my spirit rejoices in God my Savior,
for he has looked on the humble estate of his servant.
For behold, from now on all generations will call me
blessed; for he who is mighty has done great things for me,
and holy is his name.
And his mercy is for those who fear him
from generation to generation.
He has shown strength with his arm;
he has scattered the proud in the thoughts of their hearts;
he has brought down the mighty from their thrones
and exalted those of humble estate;
he has filled the hungry with good things,
and the rich he has sent away empty.
He has helped his servant Israel,
in remembrance of his mercy,
as he spoke to our fathers,
to Abraham and to his offspring forever." —Luke 1:46–55

Mary sees clearly a most remarkable thing about God: He is about to change the course of all human history. The most important three decades in all of time are about to begin.

And where is God? Occupying himself with two obscure, humble women—one old and barren (Elizabeth), one young and virginal (Mary). And Mary is so moved by this vision of God, the lover of the lowly, that she breaks out in song — a song that has come to be known as "the Magnificat" (Luke 1:46–55).

Mary and Elizabeth are wonderful heroines in Luke's account. He loves the faith of these women. The thing that impresses him most, it appears, and the thing he wants to impress on Theophilus, his noble reader, is the lowliness and cheerful humility of Elizabeth and Mary.

Elizabeth says,"Why is this granted to me that the mother of my Lord would come to me?" (Luke 1:43). And Mary says, "He has looked on the humble estate of his servant" (Luke 1:48).

The only people whose soul can truly magnify the Lord are people like Elizabeth and Mary—people who acknowledge their lowly estate and are overwhelmed by the condescension of the magnificent God.

THE LONG-AWAITED VISITATION

> *"Blessed be the Lord God of Israel, for he has visited and redeemed his people and has raised up a horn of salvation for us in the house of his servant David, as he spoke by the mouth of his holy prophets from of old, that we should be saved from our enemies and from the hand of all who hate us..."* —Luke 1:68–71

Notice two remarkable things from these words of Zechariah in Luke 1.

First, nine months earlier, Zechariah could not believe his wife would have a child. Now, filled with the Holy Spirit, he is so confident of God's redeeming work in the coming Messiah that he puts it in the past tense. For the mind of faith, a promised act of God is as good as done. Zechariah has learned to take God at his word and so has a remarkable assurance: "God has visited and redeemed!"

Second, the coming of Jesus the Messiah is a visitation

of God to our world: "The God of Israel has visited and redeemed." For centuries, the Jewish people had languished under the conviction that God had withdrawn: the spirit of prophecy had ceased, Israel had fallen into the hands of Rome. And all the godly in Israel were awaiting the visitation of God. Luke tells us in 2:25 that the devout Simeon was "looking for the consolation of Israel." And in Luke 2:38 the prayerful Anna was "looking for the redemption of Jerusalem."

These were days of great expectation. Now the long-awaited visitation of God was about to happen—indeed, he was about to come in a way no one expected.

December 4

FOR GOD'S LITTLE PEOPLE

> *In those days a decree went out from Caesar Augustus*
> *that all the world should be registered. This was the*
> *first registration when Quirinius was governor of*
> *Syria. And all went to be registered, each to his own*
> *town. And Joseph also went up from Galilee, from*
> *the town of Nazareth, to Judea, to the city of David,*
> *which is called Bethlehem, because he was of the*
> *house and lineage of David, to be registered with*
> *Mary, his betrothed, who was with child.*
> —Luke 2:1–5

Have you ever thought what an amazing thing it is that
God ordained beforehand that the Messiah be born in
Bethlehem (as the prophecy in Micah 5 shows); and that
he so ordained things that when the time came, the Messiah's mother and legal father were living in Nazareth; and
that in order to fulfill his word and bring two little people

to Bethlehem that first Christmas, God put it in the heart of Caesar Augustus that all the Roman world should be enrolled each in his own town?

Have you ever felt, like me, little and insignificant in a world of seven billion people, where all the news is of big political and economic and social movements and of outstanding people with lots of power and prestige?

If you have, don't let that make you disheartened or unhappy. For it is implicit in Scripture that all the mammoth political forces and all the giant industrial complexes, without their even knowing it, are being guided by God, not for their own sake but for the sake of God's little people—the little Mary and the little Joseph who have to be got from Nazareth to Bethlehem. God wields an empire to bless his children.

Do not think, because you experience adversity, that the hand of the Lord is shortened. It is not our prosperity but our holiness that he seeks with all his heart. And to that end, he rules the whole world. As Proverbs 21:1 says, "The king's heart is a stream of water in the hand of the Lord; he turns it wherever he will."

He is a big God for little people, and we have great cause to rejoice that, unbeknownst to them, all the kings and presidents and premiers and chancellors of the world follow the sovereign decrees of our Father in heaven, that we, the children, might be conformed to the image of his Son, Jesus Christ.

December 5

NO DETOUR FROM CALVARY

And while they were there, the time came for her to give birth. And she gave birth to her firstborn son and wrapped him in swaddling cloths and laid him in a manger, because there was no place for them in the inn. —Luke 2:6–7

Now you would think that if God so rules the world as to use an empire-wide census to bring Mary and Joseph to Bethlehem, he surely could have seen to it that a room was available in the inn.

Yes, he could have. And Jesus could have been born into a wealthy family. He could have turned stone into bread in the wilderness. He could have called 10,000 angels to his aid in Gethsemane. He could have come down from the cross and saved himself. The question is not what God *could* do, but what he *willed* to do.

God's will was that though Christ was rich, yet for your

sake he became poor. The "No Vacancy" signs over all the motels in Bethlehem were *for your sake*. "For *your* sake he became poor" (2 Corinthians 8:9).

God rules all things—even motel capacities—for the sake of his children. The Calvary road begins with a "No Vacancy" sign in Bethlehem and ends with the spitting and scoffing of the cross in Jerusalem.

And we must not forget that he said, "He who would come after me must deny himself and take up his cross" (Matthew 16:24).

We join him on the Calvary road and hear him say, "Remember the word that I said to you, 'A servant is not greater than his master.' If they persecuted me, they will persecute you" (John 15:20).

To the one who calls out enthusiastically, "I will follow you wherever you go!" (Matthew 8:19). Jesus responds, "Foxes have holes, and birds of the air have nests, but the Son of Man has nowhere to lay his head" (Matthew 8:20).

Yes, God could have seen to it that Jesus have a room at his birth. But that would have been a detour off the Calvary road.

December 6

PEACE TO THOSE WITH WHOM HE'S PLEASED

"And this will be a sign for you: you will find a baby
wrapped in swaddling cloths and lying in a manger."
And suddenly there was with the angel a multitude of
the heavenly host praising God and saying, "Glory to
God in the highest, and on earth peace among those
with whom he is pleased!" —Luke 2:12–14

Peace for whom? There is a somber note sounded in the angels' praise. Peace among men on whom his favor rests. Peace among men with whom he is pleased. Without faith it is impossible to please God. So Christmas does not bring peace to all.

"This is the judgment," Jesus said, "that the light has come into the world and men loved darkness rather than the light because their deeds are evil" (John 3:19). Or as the aged Simeon said when he saw the child Jesus, "Behold this child is set for the fall and rising of many in Israel and for a sign that is spoken against... that the thoughts of many hearts may be revealed" (Luke 2:34–35). O, how many there are who look out on a bleak and chilly Christmas day and see no more than that.

"He came to his own and his own received him not, but to as many as received him to them gave he power to become the sons of God, to as many as *believed* on his name." It was only to his disciples that Jesus said, "Peace I leave with you. My peace I give to you; not as the world gives do I give to you. Let not your heart be troubled, neither let it be afraid."

The people who enjoy the peace of God that surpasses all understanding are those who in everything by prayer and supplication let their requests be made known to God.

The key that unlocks the treasure chest of God's peace is faith in the promises of God. So Paul prays, "May the God of hope fill you with all joy and peace *in believing*" (Romans 15:13). And when we *do* trust the promises of God and have joy and peace and love, then God is glorified.

Glory to God in the highest, and on earth peace to men with whom he is pleased—men who would believe.

December 7

MESSIAH FOR THE MAGI

Now after Jesus was born in Bethlehem of Judea
in the days of Herod the king, magi from the east
arrived in Jerusalem, saying, "Where is He who has
been born King of the Jews?" —Matthew 2:1–2

Unlike Luke, Matthew does not tell us about the shepherds coming to visit Jesus in the stable. His focus is immediately on foreigners coming from the east to worship Jesus.

So Matthew portrays Jesus at the beginning and ending of his Gospel as a universal Messiah for the nations, not just for Jews.

Here the first worshipers are court magicians or astrologers or wise men not from Israel but from the East—perhaps from Babylon. They were Gentiles. Unclean.

And at the end of Matthew, the last words of Jesus are, "All authority has been given to me in heaven and on earth. Go therefore and make disciples of all the nations."

This not only opened the door for the Gentiles to rejoice in the Messiah, it added proof that he was the Messiah. Because one of the repeated prophecies was that the nations and kings would, in fact, come to him as the ruler of the world.

For example, Isaiah 60:3, "Nations will come to your light, and kings to the brightness of your rising." So Matthew adds proof to the messiahship of Jesus and shows that he is Messiah—a King, and Promise-Fulfiller—for all the nations, not just Israel.

December 8

BETHLEHEM'S SUPERNATURAL STAR

"Where is He who has been born King of the Jews?
For we saw His star in the east and have come to
worship Him." —Matthew 2:2

Over and over the Bible baffles our curiosity about just how certain things happened. How did this "star" get the magi from the east to Jerusalem?

It does not say that it led them or went before them. It only says they saw a star in the east (verse 2), and came to Jerusalem. And how did that star go before them in the little five-mile walk from Jerusalem to Bethlehem as verse 9 says it did? And how did a star stand "over the place where the Child was"?

The answer is: We do not know. There are numerous efforts to explain it in terms of conjunctions of planets or comets or supernovas or miraculous lights. We just don't know. And I want to exhort you not to become preoccupied with developing theories that are only tentative in the end and have very little spiritual significance.

I risk a generalization to warn you: People who are exercised and preoccupied with such things as how the star worked and how the Red Sea split and how the manna fell and how Jonah survived the fish and how the moon turns to blood are generally people who have what I call a mentality for the marginal. You do not see in them a deep cherishing of the great *central* things of the gospel—the holiness of God, the ugliness of sin, the helplessness of man, the death of Christ, justification by faith alone, the sanctifying work of the Spirit, the glory of Christ's return and the final judgment. They always seem to be taking you down a sidetrack with a new article or book. There is little *centered* rejoicing.

But what is plain concerning this matter of the star is that it is doing something that it cannot do on its own: it is guiding magi to the Son of God to worship him.

There is only one Person in biblical thinking that can be behind that intentionality in the stars—God himself.

So the lesson is plain: God is guiding foreigners to Christ to worship him. And he is doing it by exerting global—probably even universal—influence and power to get it done.

Luke shows God influencing the entire Roman Empire so that the census comes at the exact time to get a virgin to Bethlehem to fulfill prophecy with her delivery. Matthew shows God influencing the stars in the sky to get foreign magi to Bethlehem so that they can worship him.

This is God's design. He did it then. He is still doing it now. His aim is that the nations—all the nations (Matthew 24:14)—worship his Son.

This is God's will for everybody in your office at work, and in your neighborhood and in your home. As John 4:23 says, "Such the Father seeks to worship him."

At the beginning of Matthew we still have a "come-see" pattern. But at the end the pattern is "go-tell." The magi came and saw. We are to go and tell.

What is not different is that the purpose of God is the ingathering of the nations to worship his Son. The magnifying of Christ in the white-hot worship of all nations is the reason the world exists.

TWO KINDS OF OPPOSITION TO JESUS

When Herod the king heard this, he was troubled, and all Jerusalem with him. —Matthew 2:3

Jesus is troubling to people who do not want to worship him, and he brings out opposition for those who do. This is probably not a main point in the mind of Matthew, but it is inescapable as the story goes on.

In this story, there are two kinds of people who do not want to worship Jesus, the Messiah.

The first kind is the people who simply do nothing about Jesus. He is a nonentity in their lives. This group is represented by the chief priests and scribes. Verse 4: "Gathering together all the chief priests and scribes of the people, [Herod] inquired of them where the Messiah was to be born." Well, they told him, and that was that: back to business as usual. The sheer silence and inactivity of the leaders is overwhelming in view of the magnitude of what was happening.

And notice, verse 3 says, "When Herod the king heard this, he was troubled, and all Jerusalem with him." In other words, the rumor was going around that someone thought the Messiah was born. The inactivity on the part of chief priests is staggering—why not go with the magi? They are not interested. They do not want to worship the true God.

The second kind of people who do not want to worship Jesus is the kind who is deeply threatened by him. That is Herod in this story. He is really afraid. So much so that he schemes and lies and then commits mass murder just to get rid of Jesus.

So today these two kinds of opposition will come against Christ and his worshipers: indifference and hostility. Are you in one of those groups?

Let this Christmas be the time when you reconsider the Messiah and ponder what it is to worship him.

GOLD, FRANKINCENSE, AND MYRRH

> *When they saw the star, they rejoiced exceedingly*
> *with great joy. After coming into the house they saw*
> *the Child with Mary His mother; and they fell to*
> *the ground and worshiped Him. Then, opening*
> *their treasures, they presented to Him gifts of gold,*
> *frankincense, and myrrh.* —Matthew 2:10–11

God is not served by human hands as though he needed anything (Acts 17:25). The gifts of the magi are not given by way of assistance or need-meeting. It would dishonor a monarch if foreign visitors came with royal care-packages.

Nor are these gifts meant to be bribes. Deuteronomy 10:17 says that God takes no bribe. Well, what then do they mean? How are they worship?

The gifts are intensifiers of desire for Christ himself in much the same way that fasting is. When you give a gift to Christ like this, it's a way of saying, "The joy that I pursue (verse 10) is not the hope of getting rich with things from you. I have not come to you for your things, but for yourself. And this desire I now intensify and demonstrate by giving up things, in the hope of enjoying you more, not things. By giving to you what you do not need, and what I might enjoy, I am saying more earnestly and more authentically, 'You are my treasure, not these things.'"

I think that's what it means to worship God with gifts of gold and frankincense and myrrh.

May God take the truth of this text and waken in us a desire for Christ himself. May we say from the heart, "Lord Jesus, you are the Messiah, the King of Israel. All nations will come and bow down before you. God wields the world to see that you are worshiped. Therefore, whatever opposition I may find, I joyfully ascribe authority and dignity to you, and bring my gifts to say that you alone can satisfy my heart, not these."

December 11

WHY JESUS CAME

> *Since therefore the children share in flesh and blood,*
> *he himself likewise partook of the same things, that*
> *through death he might destroy the one who has*
> *the power of death, that is, the devil, and deliver*
> *all those who through fear of death were subject to*
> *lifelong slavery.* —Hebrews 2:14–15

Hebrews 2:14–15 is worth more than two minutes in an Advent devotional. These verses connect the beginning and the end of Jesus's earthly life. They make clear why he came. They would be great to use with an unbelieving friend or family member to take them step by step through your Christian view of Christmas. It might go something like this...

> *"Since therefore the children share in flesh and blood..."*

The term "children" is taken from the previous verse and refers to the spiritual offspring of Christ, the Messiah (see Isaiah 8:18; 53:10). These are also the "children of God." In other words, in sending Christ, God has the salvation of his "children" specially in view. It is true that "God so loved the *world*, that he sent [Jesus] (John 3:16)." But it is also true that God was *especially* "gathering the children of God who are scattered abroad" (John 11:52). God's design was to *offer* Christ to the world, and to *effect* the salvation of his "children" (see 1 Timothy 4:10). You may experience adoption by receiving Christ (John 1:12).

> *"...he himself likewise partook of the same things [flesh and blood]..."*

Christ existed before the incarnation. He was spirit. He was the eternal Word. He was with God and was God (John 1:1; Colossians 2:9). But he took on flesh and blood and clothed his deity with humanity. He became fully man and remained fully God. It is a great mystery in many ways. But it is at the heart of our faith and is what the Bible teaches.

> *"...that through death..."*

The reason Jesus became man was to die. As God, he could not die for sinners. But as man he could. His aim was to die. Therefore he had to be born human. He was born to die. Good Friday is the reason for Christmas. This is what needs to be said today about the meaning of Christmas.

"...he might destroy the one who has the power of death, that is, the devil..."

In dying, Christ de-fanged the devil. How? By covering all our sin. This means that Satan has no legitimate grounds to accuse us before God. "Who shall bring any charge against God's elect? It is God who justifies" (Romans 8:33). On what grounds does he justify? Through the blood of Jesus (Romans 5:9).

Satan's ultimate weapon against us is our own sin. If the death of Jesus takes it away, the chief weapon of the devil is taken out of his hand. He cannot make a case for our death penalty, because the Judge has acquitted us by the death of his Son!

"...and deliver all those who through fear of death were subject to lifelong slavery."

So we are free from the fear of death. God has justified us. Satan cannot overturn that decree. And God means for our ultimate safety to have an immediate effect on our lives. He means for the happy ending to take away the slavery and fear of the now.

If we do not need to fear our last and greatest enemy, death, then we do not need to fear anything. We can be free: free for joy, free for others.

What a great Christmas present from God to us! And from us to the world!

December 12

REPLACING THE SHADOWS

> *Now the main point in what has been said is this:*
> *we have such a high priest, who has taken His seat*
> *at the right hand of the throne of the Majesty in the*
> *heavens, a minister in the sanctuary, and in the true*
> *tabernacle, which the Lord pitched, not man.*
> —Hebrews 8:1–2

The point of the book of Hebrews is that Jesus Christ, God's Son, has not just come to fit into the earthly system of priestly ministry as the best and final human priest, but he has come to fulfill and put an end to that system and to orient all our attention on himself ministering for us in heaven.

The Old Testament tabernacle and priests and sacrifices were shadows. Now the reality has come, and the shadows pass away.

Here's an Advent illustration for kids (and for those of us who used to be kids and remember what it was like). Suppose you and your mom get separated in the grocery store, and you start to get scared and panic and don't know which way to go, and you run to the end of an aisle, and just before you start to cry, you see a shadow on the floor at the end of the aisle that looks just like your mom. It makes you really happy and you feel hope. But which is better? The happiness of seeing the shadow, or having your mom step around the corner and seeing that it's really her?

That's the way it is when Jesus comes to be our High Priest. That's what Christmas is. Christmas is the replacement of shadows with the real thing.

(For more on how the coming of Christ replaces the Old Testament, see the appendix at the end of this book.)

December 13

THE FINAL REALITY IS HERE

Now the main point in what has been said is this:
we have such a high priest, who has taken His seat
at the right hand of the throne of the Majesty in the
heavens, a minister in the sanctuary, and in the true
tabernacle, which the Lord pitched, not man.
—Hebrews 8:1–2

Christmas is the replacement of shadows with the real thing.

Hebrews 8:1–2 is a kind of summary statement. The point is that the one priest who goes between us and God, and makes us right with God, and prays for us to God, is not an ordinary, weak, sinful, dying, priest like in the Old Testament days. He is the Son of God—strong, sinless, with an indestructible life.

Not only that, he is not ministering in an earthly tabernacle with all its limitations of place and size and wearing out and being moth-eaten and being soaked and burned and torn and stolen. No, verse 2 says that Christ is ministering for us in a "true tabernacle, which the Lord pitched, not man." This is the real thing in heaven. This is what cast on Mount Sinai a shadow that Moses copied.

According to verse 1, another great thing about the reality which is greater than the shadow is that our High Priest is seated at the right hand of the Majesty in heaven. No Old Testament priest could ever say that.

Jesus deals directly with God the Father. He has a place of honor beside God. He is loved and respected infinitely by God. He is constantly with God. This is not shadow reality like curtains and bowls and tables and candles and robes and tassels and sheep and goats and pigeons. This is final, ultimate reality: God and his Son interacting in love and holiness for our eternal salvation.

Ultimate reality is the persons of the Godhead in relationship, dealing with each other concerning how their majesty and holiness and love and justice and goodness and truth shall be manifest in a redeemed people.

MAKING IT REAL FOR HIS PEOPLE

Christ has obtained a ministry that is as much more excellent than the old as the covenant he mediates is better, since it is enacted on better promises.
—Hebrews 8:6

Christ is the Mediator of a new covenant, according to Hebrews 8:6. What does that mean? It means that his blood—the blood of the covenant (Luke 22:20; Hebrews 13:20)—purchased the fulfillment of God's promises for us.

It means that God brings about our inner transformation by the Spirit of Christ.

And it means that God works all his transformation in us through faith in all that God is for us in Christ.

The new covenant is purchased by the blood of Christ, effected by the Spirit of Christ, and appropriated by faith in Christ.

The best place to see Christ working as the Mediator of the new covenant is in Hebrews 13:20–21:

Now the God of peace, who brought up from the dead the great Shepherd of the sheep through the blood of the eternal covenant [this is the purchase of the new covenant], even Jesus our Lord, equip you in every good thing to do His will, working in us that which is pleasing in His sight, through Jesus Christ, to whom be the glory forever and ever. Amen.

The words "working in us that which is pleasing in his sight" describe what happens when God writes the law on our hearts in the new covenant. And the words "through Jesus Christ" describe Jesus as the Mediator of this glorious work of sovereign grace.

So the meaning of Christmas is not only that God replaces shadows with Reality, but also that he takes the reality and makes it real to his people. He writes it on our hearts. He does not lay his Christmas gift of salvation and transformation down for you to pick up in your own strength. He picks it up and puts in your heart and in your mind, and seals to you that you are a child of God.

December 15

LIFE AND DEATH AT CHRISTMAS

*"The thief comes only to steal and kill and destroy.
I came that they may have life and have it
abundantly."* —John 10:10

As I was about to begin this devotional, I received word
that Marion Newstrum had just died. She and her hus-
band Elmer have been part of Bethlehem longer than
most of our members have been alive. Marion was 87. They
had been married 64 years.

When I spoke to Elmer and told him I wanted him to
be strong in the Lord and not give up on life, he said, "He
has been a true friend." I pray that all Christians will be
able to say at the end of life, "Christ has been a true friend."

Each Advent I mark the anniversary of my mother's
death. She was cut off in her 56th year in a bus accident in
Israel. It was December 16, 1974. Those events are incred-
ibly real to me even today. If I allow myself, I can easily

come to tears—for example, thinking that my sons never knew her. We buried her the day after Christmas. What a precious Christmas it was!

Many of you will feel your loss this Christmas more pointedly than before. Don't block it out. Let it come. Feel it. What is love for, if not to intensify our affections—both in life and death? But, O, do not be bitter. It is tragically self-destructive to be bitter.

Jesus came at Christmas that we might have eternal life. "I came that they might have life, and have it abundantly" (John 10:10). Elmer and Marion had discussed where they would spend their final years. Elmer said, "Marion and I agreed that our final home would be with the Lord."

Do you feel restless for home? I have family coming home for the holidays. It feels good. I think the bottom line reason for why it feels good is that they and I are destined in the depths of our being for an ultimate Homecoming. All other homecomings are foretastes. And foretastes are good.

Unless they become substitutes. O, don't let all the sweet things of this season become substitutes of the final great, all-satisfying Sweetness. Let every loss and every delight send your hearts a-homing after heaven.

Christmas. What is it but this: *I came that they might have life*. Marion Newstrum, Ruth Piper, and you and I—that we might have Life, now and forever.

Make your *Now* the richer and deeper this Christmas by drinking at the fountain of *Forever*. It is so near.

December 16

GOD'S MOST SUCCESSFUL SETBACK

"Therefore God has highly exalted him and bestowed on him the name that is above every name, so that at the name of Jesus every knee should bow, in heaven and on earth and under the earth, and every tongue confess that Jesus Christ is Lord, to the glory of God the Father." —Philippians 2:9–11

Christmas was God's most successful setback. He has always delighted to show his power through apparent defeat. He makes tactical retreats in order to win strategic victories.

Joseph was promised glory and power in his dream (Genesis 37:5–11). But to achieve that victory he had to become a slave in Egypt. And as if that were not enough, when his conditions improved because of his integrity, he was made worse than a slave — a prisoner.

But it was all planned. For there in prison he met Pharaoh's butler, who eventually brought him to Pharaoh who put him over Egypt. What an unlikely route to glory!

But that is God's way — even for his Son. He emptied himself and took the form of a slave. Worse than a slave — a prisoner — and was executed. But like Joseph, he kept his integrity. "Therefore God has highly exalted him and bestowed on him the name that is above every name, so that at the name of Jesus every knee should bow" (Philippians 2:9–10).

And this is God's way for us too. We are promised glory — if we will suffer with him (Romans 8:17). The way up is down. The way forward is backward. The way to success is through divinely appointed setbacks. They will always look and feel like failure.

But if Joseph and Jesus teach us anything this Christmas it is this: "God meant it for good!" (Genesis 50:20).

You fearful saints fresh courage take
The clouds you so much dread
Are big with mercy and will break
In blessings on your head.

December 17

THE GREATEST SALVATION
IMAGINABLE

*"Behold, the days are coming, declares the Lord, when
I will make a new covenant with the house of Israel
and the house of Judah..."* —Jeremiah 31:31

God is just and holy and separated from sinners like us.
This is our main problem at Christmas and every other
season. How shall we get right with a just and holy God?

Nevertheless, God is merciful and has promised in Jeremiah 31 (five hundred years before Christ) that someday
he would do something new. He would replace shadows
with the Reality of the Messiah. And he would powerfully
move into our lives and write his will on our hearts so that
we are not constrained from outside but are willing from
inside to love him and trust him and follow him.

That would be the greatest salvation imaginable—if
God should offer us the greatest Reality in the universe to

enjoy and then move in us to see to it that we could enjoy it with the greatest freedom and joy possible. That would be a Christmas gift worth singing about.

That is, in fact, what he promised. But there was a huge obstacle. Our sin. Our separation from God because of our unrighteousness.

How shall a holy and just God treat us sinners with so much kindness as to give us the greatest Reality in the universe (his Son) to enjoy with the greatest joy possible?

The answer is that God put our sins on his Son, and judged them there, so that he could put them out of his mind, and deal with us mercifully and remain just and holy at the same time. Hebrews 9:28 says, "Christ was offered once to bear the sins of many."

Christ bore our sins in his own body when he died. He took our judgment. He canceled our guilt. And that means the sins are gone. They do not remain in God's mind as a basis for condemnation. In that sense, he "forgets" them. They are consumed in the death of Christ.

Which means that God is now free, in his justice, to lavish us with the new covenant. He gives us Christ, the greatest Reality in the universe, for our enjoyment. And he writes his own will—his own heart—on our hearts so that we can love Christ and trust Christ and follow Christ from the inside out, with freedom and joy.

December 18

THE CHRISTMAS MODEL
FOR MISSIONS

"As you sent me into the world, so I have sent them into the world." —John 17:18

Christmas is a model for missions. Missions is a mirror of Christmas. As I, so you.

For example, danger. Christ came to his own and his own received him not. So you. They plotted against him. So you. He had no permanent home. So you. They trumped up false charges against him. So you. They whipped and mocked him. So you. He died after three years of ministry. So you.

But there is a worse danger than any of these which Jesus *escaped*. So you!

In the mid-16th century Francis Xavier (1506–1552), a Catholic missionary, wrote to Father Perez of Malacca (today part of Indonesia) about the perils of his mission to China. He said,

> *The danger of all dangers would be to lose trust and confidence in the mercy of God… To distrust him would be a far more terrible thing than any physical evil which all the enemies of God put together could inflict on us, for without God's permission neither the devils nor their human ministers could hinder us in the slightest degree.*

The greatest danger a missionary faces is to distrust the mercy of God. If that danger is avoided, then all other dangers lose their sting.

God makes every dagger a scepter in our hand. As J.W. Alexander says, "Each instant of present labor is to be graciously repaid with a million ages of glory."

Christ escaped the danger of distrust. Therefore God has highly exalted him!

Remember this Advent that Christmas is a model for missions. *As I, so you.* And that mission means danger. And that the greatest danger is distrusting God's mercy. Succumb to this, and all is lost. Conquer here, and nothing can harm you for a million ages.

December 19

CHRISTMAS IS FOR FREEDOM

Since therefore the children share in flesh and blood,
he himself likewise partook of the same things, that
through death he might destroy the one who has
the power of death, that is, the devil, and deliver
all those who through fear of death were subject to
lifelong slavery. —Hebrews 2:14–15

Jesus became man because what was needed was the death of a man who was more than man. The incarnation was God's locking himself into death row.

Christ did not risk death. He embraced it. That is precisely why he came: not to be served, but to serve, and to give his life a ransom for many (Mark 10:45).

No wonder Satan tried to turn Jesus from the cross! The cross was Satan's destruction. How did Jesus destroy him?

The "power of death" is the ability to make death fearful. The "power of death" is the power that holds men in bondage through fear of death. It is the power to keep men in sin, so that death comes as a horrid thing.

But Jesus stripped Satan of this power. He disarmed him. He molded a breastplate of righteousness for us that makes us immune to the devil's condemnation.

By his death, Jesus wiped away all our sins. And a person without sin puts Satan out of business. His treason is aborted. His cosmic treachery is foiled. "His rage we can endure, for, lo, his doom is sure." The cross has run him through. And he will gasp his last before long.

Christmas is for freedom. Freedom from the fear of death.

Jesus took our nature in Bethlehem, to die our death in Jerusalem, that we might be fearless in our city. Yes, fearless. Because if the biggest threat to my joy is gone, then why should I fret over the little ones? How can you say, "Well, I'm not afraid to die but I'm afraid to lose my job"? No. No. Think!

If death (I said, death—no pulse, cold, gone!)—if death is no longer a fear, we're free, really free. Free to take any risk under the sun for Christ and for love. No more bondage to anxiety.

If the Son has set you free, you shall be free, indeed!

December 20

CHRISTMAS SOLIDARITY

*The reason the Son of God appeared was to destroy
the works of the devil.* —1 John 3:8

The assembly line of Satan turns out millions of sins every
day. He packs them into huge cargo planes and flies them
to heaven and spreads them out before God and laughs and
laughs and laughs.

Some people work full-time on the assembly line. Others have quit their jobs there and only now and then return.

Every minute of work on the assembly line makes
God the laughing stock of Satan. Sin is Satan's business
because he hates the light and beauty and purity and
glory of God. Nothing pleases him more than when crea-
tures distrust and disobey their Maker.

Therefore, Christmas is good news for man and good
news for God.

"The saying is sure and worthy of full acceptance, that Christ Jesus came into the world to save sinners" (1 Timothy 1:15). That's good news for us.

"The reason the Son of God appeared was to destroy the works of the devil" (1 John 3:8). That's good news for God.

Christmas is good news for God because Jesus has come to lead a strike at Satan's assembly plant. He has walked right into the plant, called for the Solidarity of the faithful, and begun a massive walk-out.

Christmas is a call to go on strike at the assembly plant of sin. No negotiations with the management. No bargaining. Just single-minded, unswerving opposition to the product.

Christmas Solidarity aims to ground the cargo planes. It will not use force or violence, but with relentless devotion to Truth it will expose the life-destroying conditions of the devil's industry.

Christmas Solidarity will not give up until a complete shutdown has been achieved.

When sin has been destroyed, God's name will be wholly exonerated. No one will be laughing at him anymore.

If you want to give a gift to God this Christmas, walk off the assembly line and never go back. Take up your place in the picket line of love. Join Christmas Solidarity until the majestic name of God is cleared and he stands glorious amid the accolades of the righteous.

THE BIRTH OF THE ANCIENT OF DAYS

> *Then Pilate said to him, "So you are a king?" Jesus*
> *answered, "You say that I am a king. For this purpose*
> *I was born and for this purpose I have come into the*
> *world—to bear witness to the truth. Everyone who is*
> *of the truth listens to my voice."* —John 18:37

This is a great Christmas text even though it comes from
the end of Jesus's life on earth, not the beginning.

The uniqueness of his birth is that he did not originate
at his birth. He existed before he was born in a manger. The
personhood, the character, the personality of Jesus of Nazareth existed before the man Jesus of Nazareth was born.

The theological word to describe this mystery is not *cre-
ation*, but *incarnation*. The person—not the body, but the
essential personhood of Jesus—existed before he was born
as man. His birth was not a coming into being of a new person, but a coming into the world of an infinitely old person.

Micah 5:2 puts it like this, 700 years before Jesus was born:

> But you, O Bethlehem Ephrathah, who are too little to be among the clans of Judah, from you shall come forth for me one who is to be ruler in Israel, whose coming forth is from of old, from ancient days.

The mystery of the birth of Jesus is not merely that he was born of a virgin. That miracle was intended by God to witness to an even greater one—namely, that the child born at Christmas was a person who existed "from of old, from ancient days."

December 22

THAT YOU MAY BELIEVE

Now Jesus did many other signs in the presence of
the disciples, which are not written in this book; but
these are written so that you may believe that Jesus is
the Christ, the Son of God, and that by believing you
may have life in his name. —John 20:30–31

I feel so strongly that among those of us who have grown
up in church and who can recite the great doctrines of
our faith in our sleep and who yawn through the Apostles
Creed—that among us something must be done to help
us once more feel the awe, the fear, the astonishment, the
wonder of the Son of God, begotten by the Father from
all eternity, reflecting all the glory of God, being the very
image of his person, through whom all things were created,
upholding the universe by the word of his power.

You can read every fairy tale that was ever written, every
mystery thriller, every ghost story, and you will never find

anything so shocking, so strange, so weird and so spell-binding as the story of the incarnation of the Son of God.

How dead we are! How callous and unfeeling to his glory and his story! How often have I had to repent and say, "God, I am sorry that the stories men have made up stir my emotions, my awe and wonder and admiration and joy, more than your own true story."

The space thrillers of our day, like *Star Wars* and *The Empire Strikes Back*, can do this great good for us: they can humble us and bring us to repentance, by showing us that we really are capable of some of the wonder and awe and amazement that we so seldom feel when we contemplate the eternal God and the cosmic Christ and a real living contact between them and us in Jesus of Nazareth.

When Jesus said, "For this I have come into the world," he said something as crazy and weird and strange and eerie as any statement in science fiction that you have ever read (John 18:37).

O, how I pray for a breaking forth of the Spirit of God upon me and upon you. I pray for the Holy Spirit to break into my experience in a frightening way, to wake me up to the unimaginable reality of God.

One of these days lightning is going to fill the sky from the rising of the sun to its setting, and there is going to appear in the clouds one like a son of man with his mighty angels in flaming fire. And we will see him clearly. And whether from terror or sheer excitement, we will tremble and we will wonder how, how we ever lived so long with such a domesticated, harmless Christ.

These things are written that you might believe that Jesus Christ is the Son of God who came into the world. *Really* believe.

December 23

GOD'S INDESCRIBABLE GIFT

*If while we were enemies we were reconciled to God
by the death of his Son, much more, now that we
are reconciled, shall we be saved by his life. More
than that, we also rejoice in God through our Lord
Jesus Christ, through whom we have now received
reconciliation.* —Romans 5:10–11

How do we practically receive reconciliation and exult in
God? One answer is: do it through Jesus Christ. Which
means, at least in part, make the portrait of Jesus in the
Bible—the work and the words of Jesus portrayed in the
New Testament—the essential content of your exultation
over God. Exultation without the content of Christ does
not honor Christ.

In 2 Corinthians 4:4–6, Paul describes conversion two
ways. In verse 4, he says it is seeing "the glory of Christ,
who is the image of God." And in verse 6, he says it is seeing

"the glory of God in the face of Jesus Christ." In either case you see the point. We have Christ, the image of God, and we have God in the face of Christ.

Practically, to exult in God, you exult in what you see and know of God in the portrait of Jesus Christ. And this comes to its fullest experience when the love of God is poured out in our hearts by the Holy Spirit, as Romans 5:5 says.

So here's the Christmas point. Not only did God purchase our reconciliation through the death of the Lord Jesus Christ (verse 10), and not only did God enable us to receive that reconciliation through the Lord Jesus Christ (verse 11), but even now, verse 11 says, we exult in God himself through our Lord Jesus Christ.

Jesus purchased our reconciliation. Jesus enabled us to receive the reconciliation and open the gift. And Jesus himself shines forth from the wrapping—the indescribable gift—as God in the flesh, and stirs up all our exultation in God.

Look to Jesus this Christmas. Receive the reconciliation that he bought. Don't put it on the shelf unopened. And don't open it and then make it a means to all your other pleasures.

Open it and enjoy the gift. Exult in him. Make him your pleasure. Make him your treasure.

THE SON OF GOD APPEARED

Little children, make sure no one deceives you; the one who practices righteousness is righteous, just as He is righteous; the one who practices sin is of the devil; for the devil has sinned from the beginning. The Son of God appeared for this purpose, to destroy the works of the devil. —1 John 3:7–8

When verse 8 says, "The Son of God appeared for this purpose, to destroy the works of the devil," what are the "works of the devil" that he has in mind? The answer is clear from the context.

First, verse 5 is a clear parallel: "You know that He appeared in order to take away sins." The phrase "he appeared to..." occurs in verse 5 and verse 8. So probably the "works of the devil" that Jesus came to destroy are sins. The first part of verse 8 makes this virtually certain:

"The one who practices sin is of the devil; for the devil has sinned from the beginning."

The issue in this context is sinning, not sickness or broken cars or messed up schedules. Jesus came into the world to help us stop sinning.

Let me put it alongside the truth of 1 John 2:1: "My little children, I am writing these things to you so that you may not sin." In other words, I am promoting the purpose of Christmas (3:8), the purpose of the incarnation. Then he adds (2:2), "And if anyone sins, we have an Advocate with the Father, Jesus Christ the righteous, and He Himself is the propitiation for our sins; and not for ours only, but also for those of the whole world."

But now look what this means: It means that Jesus appeared in the world for two reasons. He came that we might not go on sinning; and he came to die so that there would be a propitiation—a substitutionary sacrifice that takes away the wrath of God—for our sins, if we do sin.

December 25

THREE CHRISTMAS PRESENTS

Little children, make sure no one deceives you; the one who practices righteousness is righteous, just as He is righteous; the one who practices sin is of the devil; for the devil has sinned from the beginning. The Son of God appeared for this purpose, to destroy the works of the devil. —1 John 3:7–8

Ponder this remarkable situation with me. If the Son of God came to help you stop sinning—to destroy the works of the devil—and if he also came to die so that, when you do sin, there is a propitiation, a removal of God's wrath, then what does this imply for living your life?

Three things. And they are wonderful to have. I give them to you briefly as Christmas presents.

1. A Clear Purpose for Living

It implies that you have a clear purpose for living. Negatively, it is simply this: don't sin. "I write these things to you so that you may not sin" (1 John 2:1). "The Son of God appeared to destroy the works of the devil" (1 John 3:8).

If you ask, "Can you give us that positively, instead of negatively?" the answer is: Yes, it's all summed up in 1 John 3:23. It's a great summary of what John's whole letter requires. Notice the singular "commandment"—"This is His commandment, that we believe in the name of His Son Jesus Christ, and love one another, just as He commanded us." These two things are so closely connected for John he calls them one commandment: believe Jesus and love others. That is your purpose. That is the sum of the Christian life. Trusting Jesus, loving people. Trust Jesus, love people. There's the first gift: a purpose to live.

2. Hope That Our Failures Will Be Forgiven

Now consider the second implication of the twofold truth that Christ came to destroy our sinning and to forgive our sins. It's this: We make progress in overcoming our sin when we have hope that our failures will be forgiven. If you don't have hope that God will forgive your failures, when you start fighting sin, you give up.

Many of you are pondering some changes in the new year, because you have fallen into sinful patterns and want out. You want some new patterns of eating. New patterns for entertainment. New patterns of giving. New patterns of relating to your spouse. New patterns of family devotions. New patterns of sleep and exercise. New patterns of courage in witness. But you are struggling, wondering whether it's any use. Well here's your second Christmas present: Christ not only came to destroy the works of the devil—our sinning— he also came to be an advocate for us when we fail in our fight.

So I plead with you, let the freedom to fail give you the hope to fight. But beware! If you turn the grace of God into license, and say, "Well, if I can fail, and it doesn't matter, then why bother fighting?"—if you say that, and mean it, and go on acting on it, you are probably not born again and should tremble.

But that is not where most of you are. Most of you want to fight sinful patterns in your life. And what God is saying to you is this: Let the freedom to fail give you hope to fight. I write this to you that you might not sin, but if you sin you have an advocate, Jesus Christ.

3. Christ Will Help Us

Finally, the third implication of the double truth that Christ came to destroy our sinning and to forgive our sins, is this: Christ will really help us in our fight. He really will help you. He is on your side. He didn't come to destroy sin because sin is fun. He came to destroy sin because it is fatal. It is a deceptive work of the devil and will destroy us if we don't fight it. He came to help us, not hurt us.

So here's your third Christmas gift: Christ will help overcome sin in you. 1 John 4:4 says, "He who is in you is greater than he that is in the world." Jesus is alive, Jesus is almighty, Jesus lives in us by faith. And Jesus is for us, not against us. He will help you. Trust him.

Conclusion

MY FAVORITE CHRISTMAS TEXT

My favorite Christmas text puts humility at the heart of Christmas. So this Christmas I am marveling at Jesus's humility and wanting more of it myself. I'll quote the text in a moment.

But first there are two problems. Tim Keller helps us to see one of them when he says, "Humility is so shy. If you begin talking about it, it leaves." So a meditation on humility (like this one) is self-defeating, it seems. But even shy people peek out sometimes if they are treated well.

The other problem is that Jesus wasn't humble for the same reasons we are (or should be). So how can looking at Jesus's Christmas humility help us? Our humility, if there is any at all, is based on our finiteness, our fallibility, and our sinfulness. But the eternal Son of God was not finite. He was not fallible. And he was not sinful. So, unlike our humility, Jesus' humility originated some other way.

Here is my favorite Christmas text. Look for Jesus's humility.

> *Though he was in the form of God, [Jesus] did not*
> *count equality with God a thing to be grasped, but*
> *made himself nothing, taking the form of a servant,*
> *being born in the likeness of men. And being found*
> *in human form, he humbled himself by becoming*
> *obedient to the point of death, even death on a cross.*
> *(Philippians 2:6–8)*

What defines Jesus's humility is the fact that it is mainly a conscious act of putting himself in a lowly, servant role for the good of others. His humility is defined by phrases like

› "he emptied himself [of his divine rights to be free from abuse and suffering]"

› "he took the form of a servant"

› "he became obedient to the point of death, even death on a cross"

So Jesus's humility was not a heart disposition of being finite or fallible or sinful. It was a heart of infinite perfection and infallible truthfulness and freedom from all sin, which for that very reason did not need to be served. He was free and full to overflow in serving.

Another Christmas text that says this would be Mark 10:45: "The Son of Man came *not to be served* but *to serve*, and to give his life as a ransom for many." Jesus's humility was not a sense of defect in himself, but a sense of fullness in himself put at the disposal of others for their good. It was a voluntary lowering of himself to make the height of his glory available for sinners to enjoy.

Jesus makes the connection between his Christmas

lowliness and the good news for us: "Come to me, all who labor and are heavy laden, and I will give you rest. Take my yoke upon you, and learn from me, for I am gentle and *lowly in heart*, and you will find rest for your souls. For my yoke is easy, and my burden is light" (Matthew 11:28–30).

His lowliness makes our relief from burdens possible. If he were not lowly, he would not have been "obedient unto death, even death on a cross." And if he had not been obedient to die for us, we would be crushed under the weight of our sins. He lowers himself to take our condemnation (Romans 8:3).

Now we have more reason to be humble than before. We are finite, fallible, sinful, and therefore have no ground for boasting at all. But now we see other humbling things: Our salvation is not owing to our work, but his grace. So boasting is excluded (Ephesians 2:8–9). And the way he accomplished that gracious salvation was through voluntary, conscious self-lowering in servant-like obedience to the point of death.

So in addition to finiteness, fallibility, and sinfulness, we now have two other huge impulses at work to humble us: free and undeserved grace underneath all our blessings and a model of self-denying, sacrificial, servanthood that willingly takes the form of a servant.

So we are called to join Jesus in this conscious self-humbling and servanthood. "Whoever exalts himself will be humbled, and whoever humbles himself will be exalted" (Matthew 23:12). "Have this mind among yourselves, which is yours in Christ Jesus..." (Philippians 2:5).

Let's pray that this "shy virtue"—this massive ground of our salvation and our servanthood—would peek out from her quiet place and grant us the garments of lowliness this Advent. "Clothe yourselves, all of you, with humility toward one another, for 'God opposes the proud but gives grace to the humble'" (1 Peter 5:5).

OLD TESTAMENT SHADOWS AND THE COMING OF CHRIST

One of the main points of the book of Hebrews is that the Old Covenant system of worship is a shadow replaced by Christ. So Christmas is the replacement of shadows with reality. (You can see this in Hebrews 8:5 where it says that the priests "serve a *copy and shadow* of the heavenly things.")

Consider six such shadows that the coming of Christ replaces with reality.

1 **The shadow of the Old Covenant priesthood.** "And the former priests, on the one hand, existed in greater numbers, because they were prevented by death from continuing, but he, on the other hand, because he abides forever, holds his priesthood permanently" (Hebrews 7:23–24).

2 **The shadow of the Passover sacrifice.** "Clean out the old leaven, that you may be a new lump, just as you are in fact unleavened. For Christ our Passover also has been sacrificed" (1 Corinthians 5:7).

3 **The shadow of the tabernacle and temple.** "Now the main point in what has been said is this: we have such a high priest, who has taken his seat at the right hand of the throne of the Majesty in the heavens, a minister in the sanctuary, and in the true tabernacle, which the Lord pitched, not man" (Hebrews 8:1–2).

"Jesus answered and said to them, 'Destroy this temple, and in three days I will raise it up.' The Jews therefore said, 'It took forty-six years to build this temple, and will you raise it up in three days?' But he was speaking of the temple of his body" (John 2:19–21).

4 **The shadow of circumcision.** "Circumcision is nothing, and uncircumcision is nothing, but what matters is the keeping of the commandments of God" (1 Corinthians 7:19).

5 **The shadow of dietary laws.** "And he said to them, 'Are you so lacking in understanding also? Do you not understand that whatever goes into the man from outside cannot defile him; because it does not go into his heart, but into his stomach and is eliminated?' (Thus he declared all foods clean.)" (Mark 7:18–19).

6 **The shadow of feast days.** "Therefore let no one act as your judge in regard to food or drink or in respect to a festival or a new moon or a Sabbath day—things which are a mere shadow of what is to come; but the substance belongs to Christ" (Colossians 2:16–17).

The meaning of Christmas is that the substance belongs to Christ. That is, religious ritual is like a shadow of a great and glorious Person. Let us turn from the shadow and look the Person in the face (2 Corinthians 4:6). My little children, keep yourselves from (religious) idols (1 John 5:21).

❊ desiringGod

The mission of Desiring God is that people everywhere would understand and embrace the truth that God is most glorified in us when we are most satisfied in him. Our primary strategy for accomplishing this mission is through a maximally useful website that houses over thirty years of John Piper's preaching and teaching, including translations into more than 40 languages. This is all available free of charge, thanks to our generous ministry partners. If you would like to further explore the vision of Desiring God, we encourage you to visit www.desiringGod.org.

Desiring God

Post Office Box 2901, Minneapolis, Minnesota 55402
888.346.4700   mail@desiringGod.org

6087804R00044

Made in the USA
San Bernardino, CA
30 November 2013